Cars

American Retro

SOURCEBOOKS, INC.®
NAPERVILLE, ILLINOIS

Cars

American Retro

Stop dreaming
and start living.

'50s car ad

Contents

Introduction

"On that road the nation is steadily traveling beyond the troubles of this century, constantly heading toward finer tomorrows. The American Road is paved with hope."

1951 Ford ad

The great highways of America were its very heart and soul. They spanned the limits of this vast country from top to bottom and east to west. They carried the new breed of motorists from good to bad, from boom to bust, through towns with such names as Mammoth Cave, Kentucky; Pleasantville, New York; and Broken Bow, Nebraska; many of them with nothing more than a Main Street and a drugstore.

Along the way these arteries offered succor in the form of welcoming diners, serving plates of wholesome freshly prepared dishes—food that spawned a universal language in the shape of hot dogs, hamburgers, fries, and malts. Comfortable motels with warm rooms offered the latest in modern conveniences, from power showers to the combination television and radio set, and provided a safe haven for the night. They were clean and affordable family businesses, which allowed the nuclear family, for the first time, to explore the wonders of their own land.

Parked outside were the trappings of prosperity—Cadillacs, T-Birds, Chevrolets, and Corvettes—cars that any sane person has always wanted to drive. These were elongated giants, explosions of chrome grilles and wire wheels, creating fantasies of speed and escapism with features taken from aircraft designs and space travel. These were the only beasts capable of taming this extraordinary country, and are as representative of the United States of America as the Statue of Liberty or the Stars and Stripes.

The names of those great roads—Highway 61, Route 66, Pacific 1—have since passed into popular mythology. For those with a passion for adventure, the names evoke images of *Easy Rider*, and the lyrics of Bob Dylan and the Rolling Stones. At the same time, they are able to convey that air of safety and innocence, when mom and pop ushered the kids into the back of the family automobile and headed off on vacation.

Now this golden age is all but gone, although remnants do remain. The highways have fallen into disrepair, superseded by freeways with no recognizable character. Many diners have served their last "special," and a large number of "ma and pa" motels have been swallowed up into chains with such alluring names as Comfort Inn and Motel 6 (we are never told what happened to Motels 1 through 5). Small towns, with the whole of life encapsulated on Main Street, are a far cry from the soulless shopping malls of today. And the cars—oh those glorious, gas-guzzling monsters—have been replaced by sensible, compact, economical models with dull names.

As a tribute to the post-war period when people had money in their pockets and a hankering to spend it, the four titles in the *American Retro* series draw on images, both retro and modern, that resonate with the spirit of '50s America. These pictures are paired with advertising slogans, popular sayings, puns, and quotations from personalities that bring to life an age when being economical with the truth came naturally to the advertisers and salesmen of the day, who were desperate to paint a dazzling and futuristic world in which everyone could share. Motels shamelessly claimed to offer comfort fit for the "Queen of Sheba"; car manufacturers used such buzz words as "Rocket Ride" and "Glamorous new Futuramics"; and diners bedecked themselves in chrome detailing and neon lights.

The *American Retro* series recaptures a little of what made those times so special, with images that will fill those who lived through that age with nostalgia and gently amuse and inform those who did not. Read, remember, and enjoy.

This baby can flick its tail

at anything on the road.

Ford Thunderbird

The car everyone

would love to own!

Outer beauty reflects inner quality.

What does your car say about you?

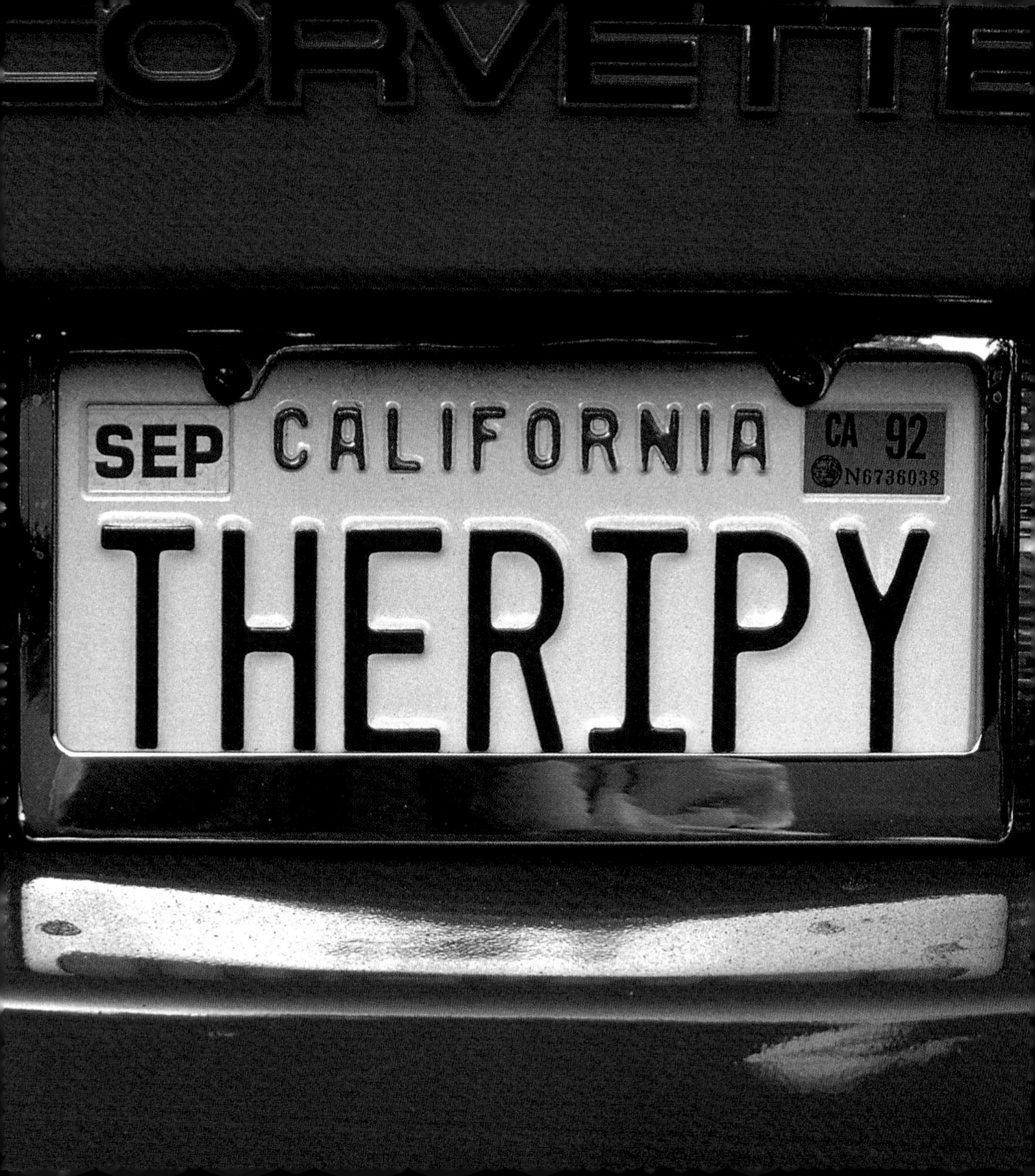
CORVETTE
SEP
CALIFORNIA
CA 92
N6736038
THERIPY

A masterpiece from a master craftsman.

"Start packing—we're moving out," said the man to his wife.

"Moving, dear?" she replied, "It's four in the morning."

Her husband sat down wearily and explained.

Everyone else in the neighborhood could afford a new Dodge.

Dodge sedan

More people named Jones

own Chevrolets than

any other car!

(are you keeping up

with the Joneses?)

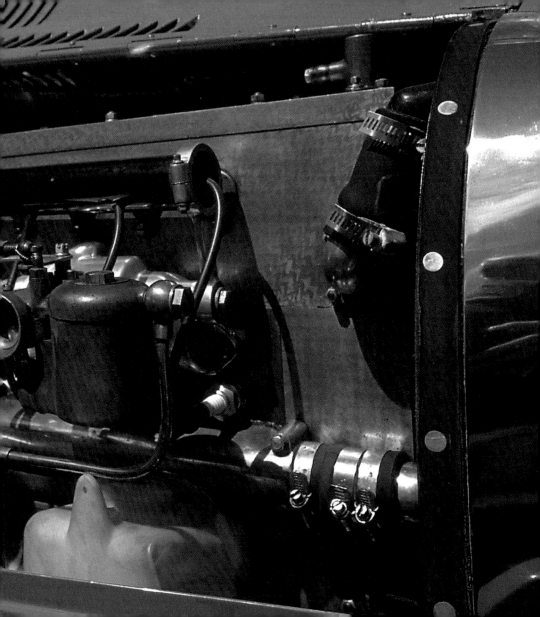

See the USA

in your Chevrolet.

'55 Chevrolet

Driving is a spectacular
form of amnesia.

Everything is to be
discovered,
everything to be
obliterated.

Jean Baudrillard

A fine car appeals to me as much as a good horse.

'37 Packard convertible

Dispense with a horse

and get a Mustang.

CALIFORNIA

STUDE 51

We were impressed with fighter aircraft and wanted to impart some of that flavor to the Studebaker.

Robert Bourke

Stop dreaming

and start living.

Tail fins of '50s Cadillacs

There's a Ford in your future.

'32 Ford pickup truck

Any color

as long as it's not black.

'34 Ford

Escape from the ordinary.

Plymouth builds great cars.

Hood of a '40s Plymouth

Automobiles mean progress
for our country,

greater happiness,

and greater
standards of living.

Dwight D. Eisenhower

'47 Ford convertible

We're not the richest

people in town...

but we're the proudest!

My husband knows all about engines and brakes

but I'm the expert on style!

Cadillac

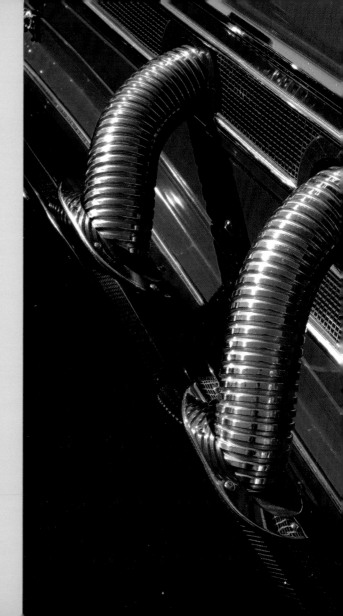

Women judge a car mostly on its beauty,

comfort, safety, ease of handling, and its perfection in detail.

To men—power, economy, and how it's put together are most important.

We do not

remember days;

we remember moments.

'59 Cadillac convertible

Door handle to a vintage Hot Rod

Make a little thunder
of your own.

'57 Ford Thunderbird

Chevy can match

your personality

and then some!

'57 Chevrolet convertible

I'm going to build a car

for the multitude.

Henry Ford

What's great about this country is that America started the tradition where the richest consumers buy essentially the same things as the poorest.

Andy Warhol

Elvis's car

Dreams on wheels.

Reflection of a vintage Hot Rod

America's only true sports car.

Corvette convertible

Cadillac...

world's synonym for quality!

'59 Harley Earl Cadillac

The man who goes alone can start today;

but he who travels with another must wait 'til that other is ready.

Henry David Thoreau

Hood ornament on a '57 Chevrolet 87

Style alone does not

make a motor-car.

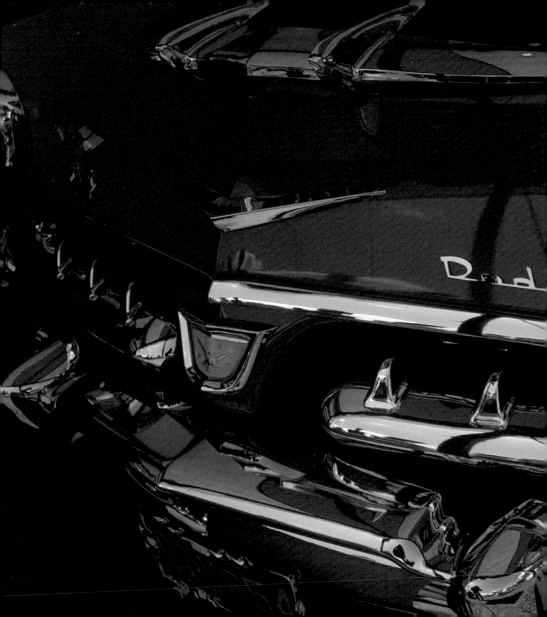

Darling,

they're staring

at our new Dodge.

Tell me how a man drives,

and I will tell you

what kind of man he is.

Ernest Dichter

If you can't drive a
police car,

at least
get a ride in one.

SEP **Washington** '93
389 - BTJ
· Centennial Celebration ·

Pontiac—

more style,

more power,

And a built-in future.

Full of spunk...

but beautifully behaved

...the '57 Chevy.

The young people of our world are turned on and tuned in to life.

To its mood and music.

To its adventure and excitement.

How to catch a Thunderbird...

Find one that's standing still.

In full flight this is a most elusive species with a rare talent

for disappearing from the view of lesser cars.

That new V-8 in the '57 Chevrolet

is as quiet as a contented cat

and as smooth as cream.

Front end of a '57 Chevrolet

Oldsmobile rockets ahead!

Picture credits

Page 8/9: Pink classic car parked on Ocean Drive, Miami Beach, Florida; credit Franz-Marc Frei

Page 10/11: Classic Thunderbirds in Occidental, California; credit Morton Beebe.

Page 12/13: Hood ornament on a '55 Chevrolet sedan in Temecula, California; credit Richard Cummins.

Page 14/15: Vanity plate on a Corvette in Los Angeles, California; credit Annie Griffiths Belt.

Page 16/17: Vintage Cadillac in Port Orchard, Washington; credit Neil Rabinowitz.

Page 18/19: Dashboard of an antque automobile in Washington; credit Neil Rabinowitz.

Page 20/21: '60s Dodge sedan in Kingman, Arizona; credit Wild Country.

Page 22/23: Rust colored vintage Chevrolet in Redwood City, California; credit Henry Diltz.

Page 24/25: 1954 Chevy pickup truck in Maryland; credit Annie Griffiths Belt.

Page 26/27: Classic car engine in Pebble Beach, California; credit Joseph Sohm.

Page 28/29: '55 Chevrolet with the Maryland "Bobby-55" licence plate; credit Joseph Sohm.

Page 30/31: Car on the highway in Abiquiu, New Mexico; credit Macduff Everton.

Page 32/33: Old gas station in Texas; credit Joseph Sohm.

Page 34/35: '37 Packard convertible; credit Robert Dowling.

Page 36/37: A Virginia vanity licence plate on a Mustang; credit Joseph Sohm.

Page 38/39: Headlamp of a vintage car in South Miami Beach, Florida; credit The Purcell Team.

Page 40/41: '51 Studebaker convertible in Los Angeles, California.

Page 42/43: Fins of '50s Cadillacs in Beverly Hills, California; credit Joseph Sohm.

Page 44/45: Headlight of a '37 Ford pickup truck in Pomona, California; credit Richard Cummins.

Page 46/47: '34 Fords in Temecula, California; credit Richard Cummins.

Page 48/49: Arizona licence plate; credit Reinhard Eisele.

Page 50/51: Hood of a '40s Plymouth in Washington; credit Kevin R. Morris.

Page 52/53: Headlight of '47 Ford convertible; credit Richard Cummins.

Page 54/55: Vintage Plymouth in Los Angeles, California; credit Henry Diltz.

Page 56/57: American classic cars on Ocean Drive, Miami Beach, Florida; reproduced by permission of Travel Ink/Abbie Enock.

Page 58/59: Cadillac filling up a a Texaco station in New Orleans, Louisiana; credit Charles E. Rotkin.

Page 60/61: Classic car engine pipes in Palm Springs, California; credit Mark Stephenson.

Page 62/63: '59 Cadillac convertible on Sunset Boulevard, Los Angeles, California; credit Joseph Sohm.

Page 64/65: Automobile lights on a road in Alaska; credit Patrick Bennett.

Page 66/67: Door handle on a vintage Hot Rod in Temecula, California; credit Richard Cummins.

Page 68/69: Interior of a '57 Ford Thunderbird in Orange County, California; credit Richard Cummins.

Page 70/71: '57 Chevrolet convertible with a Washington licence plate; credit Joseph Sohm.

Page 72/73: Ford F-100 Trademark; credit Richard Cummins.

Page 74/75: Ford convertible outside a general store; credit Robert Dowling.

Page 76/77: Elvis's car in Memphis, Tennessee; credit Todd Gipstein.

Page 78/79: Reflection in hubcap of a vintage Hot Rod; credit Richard Cummins.

Page 80/81: Classic convertible Corvette in California; credit Vince Streano.

Page 82/83: '59 Harley Earl Cadillac in Arizona; credit Robert Dowling.

Page 84/85: Car on a gravel road; credit Richard Hamilton Smith.

Page 86/87: Hood ornament on a '57 Chevrolet in Orange County, California; credit Richard Cummins.

Page 88/89: Dashboard of a vintage automobile in Washington; credit Neil Rabinowitz.

Page 90/91: Grille of a '56 Dodge in Macunige, Pennsylvania; credit John Bartholomew.

Page 92/93: Personalized California plate; credit Joseph Sohm.

Page 94/95: Police car in California; credit Tim Page.

Page 96/97: '65 Pontiac GTO in Washington; credit Neil Rabinowitz.

Page 98/99: '57 Chevrolet on Miami Beach, Florida; credit Joseph Sohm.

Page 100/101: Interior of a '52 Buick; credit John Bartholomew.

Page 102/103: Classic Thunderbirds in Occidental, California; credit Morton Beebe.

Page 104/105: Front end of '57 Chevrolet in Orange County, California; credit Richard Cummins.

Page 106/107: Classic Oldsmobile in Sausalito, California; credit Robert Holmes.

Attributions

Designer: WDA
Editor: Alison Moss
Researcher: Suzie Green

Sourcebooks, Inc.
P.O. Box 4410, Naperville, Illinois 60567-4410
(630) 961-3900
FAX: (630) 961-2168

Printed and bound in Spain by Bookprint, S.L, Barcelona

MQ 10 9 8 7 6 5 4 3 2 1

ISBN: 1-57071-592-0